Introduction

Jump on the knitting bandwagon and make yourself and a loved one a warm and cozy item with a circular knitting loom. It's easy to master by crafters of all ages.

Keep-Warm Hat and Tubular Scarf are great starter projects. They will introduce you to knitting in the round on a loom. Make-It-Soft Hat & Scarf are made of luscious soft suede-like yarn.

The thick, cozy pair of At-Home-Comfort Socks is sure to keep your tootsies warm even on the coldest nights. Mom & Daughter Bangle Bags have their handles knit right into the design. Knit the large one for everyday and the small one for your daughter or for an evening out!

Pleasing Ponchette has versatile style for evening or everyday casual. It's a great addition to your wardrobe!

Striped Squares Baby Blanket is a wonderful gift to welcome the next baby in your life. A warm and cozy Relaxing Afghan is knit in your choice of three colors to match your home decor. It will keep you or that special someone comfy on a cool evening.

All of these easy knitting loom projects are fun and sure to be a hit with your friends and family!

Design Directory

General Directions

Materials

Knifty Knitter looms from Provo Craft (Our photo-graphed items were designed with the Knifty Knitter circle looms. Although you can use other circular looms, such as the In the Attic Looms, the gauge may be slightly off.)
Knitting tool
Crochet hook
Yarn needle

Techniques

Casting On

1. Tie a slip knot at the end of your yarn (check the pattern for the number of strands to be wrapped), leaving a 3-inch tail. Place this knot on the holding peg, and pull gently to tighten, **Photo 1**.

Note: *After knitting two rows, the slip knot should be removed from the holding peg.*

2. With your working yarn held in your left hand on the inside of the loom, wrap each peg in a counterclock-wise direction starting on the first peg to the left of the holding peg. Work your way around the loom, going in a clockwise direction until there is one loop on each peg. Don't wrap too tightly, **Photo 2**.

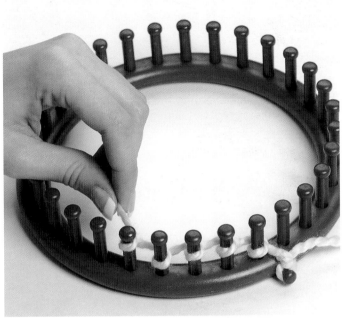

Photo 2

Photo 1

3. Work your way around the loom sliding each loop halfway down each peg.

4. Continue to wrap your working yarn around the loom a second time until there are two loops on each peg.

Basic Stitches

Knitting on a knitting loom yields results similar to those of knitting with circular needles. The basic stitches used on the knitting loom are the Knit Stitch and the Purl Stitch. Alternating rows of these two stitches will result in a garter stitch that is the same on both sides of the piece.

Knit Stitch

1. Cast on and wrap two loops on number of pegs as directed in the pattern.

2. Start with the first peg to the left of your holding peg. Use your knitting tool to take the bottom loop and pull it up and over the top loop and over the top of the peg, **Photo 3**.

Photo 3

3. Continue in this manner, working in a clockwise direction around the loom until all pegs only have one loop remaining on them. This is one round.

Purl Stitch

1. Wrap one loop on number of pegs as directed in the pattern.

2. Lay your working yarn across the front of the pegs, just below the first wrapped loop, **Photo 4**.

Photo 4

3. Using your knitting tool, reach down through the wrapped loop on the first peg and pull the working yarn up through the loop, forming another loop, **Photo 5**.

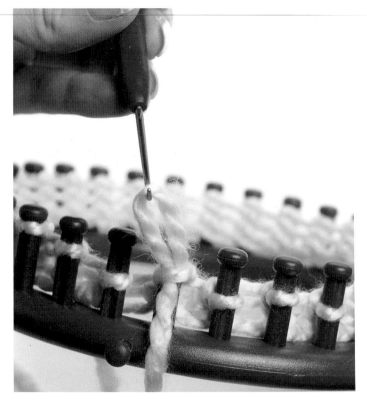

Photo 5

4. Pull the original wrapped loop off the peg, **Photo 6**, and place the newly formed loop on the peg. Tug gently on the working yarn to secure the loop on the peg.

Photo 6

5. Move to the next peg and repeat stitch as called for in the pattern.

Garter Stitch

1. Wrap the number of pegs as directed in the pattern until there are two loops on each peg and knit off one row.

2. The next row is done in purl stitch.

3. Alternate the rows in stockinette stitch and purl stitches as called for in the pattern. This creates a garter-stitch-look in your work.

Knitting a Flat Piece

1. Working around the loom clockwise, cast on the amount of stitches as directed in the pattern.

2. Wrap the last peg twice counter clockwise and bring your working yarn behind the next peg to the right. Wrap the yarn clockwise around the peg, **Photo 7**.

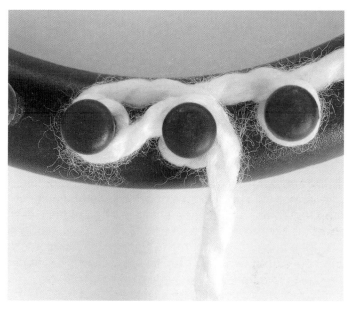

Photo 7

3. Continue to wrap the yarn around each peg clockwise working back toward the holding peg.

4. Starting with the last peg wrapped, knit off all pegs. The working yarn will be on the right end of the row.

Note: *The stitch on the last peg that was double wrapped will be loose.*

5. The working yarn will be *behind* the first peg on the right. Bring the yarn around to the front of the first peg wrapping in a counterclockwise direction.

6. Continue wrapping all pegs, working in a clockwise direction on the loom and knit off, again starting with the last peg that was wrapped.

7. Continue in this manner wrapping the pegs back and forth on the loom as directed in the pattern.

Note: *Remember each peg will be wrapped clockwise as you move from left to right. Then they will be wrapped counterclockwise as you move right to left on the piece.*

Purling on a Flat Piece

1. Cast on and wrap as many pegs as directed in pattern working in a clockwise direction.

2. Wrap the last peg and bring the working yarn around the left side of the last peg and in front of the peg just below the first loop.

3. Using your knitting tool, reach down through the wrapped loop on the first peg, and pull the working yarn up and through the loop, forming another loop.

4. Pull the original wrapped loop off the peg, and place the newly formed loop on the peg. Tug gently on the working yarn to secure the loop on the peg.

5. Continue to purl to the end of the row or as directed in the pattern.

Bind Off

There are four ways to bind off your finished piece: gather method, flat piece method, tube method and flat closed method. The gather method can be used to close up items like the tops of hats where the piece is a tube and then one end is gathered to close it. The flat piece method is used when making flat pieces such as scarves or afghan panels. The tube method can be used for items such as sleeves, where a circular piece is desired and both ends need to be left open. Flat closed method is used when knitting a piece in the round and a straight bottom is desired such as for a bag or pouch.

Note: It is helpful to have a crochet hook for some bind off methods; otherwise the knitting tool can be used.

Gather Method

1. Once the piece reaches the desired length, wrap your working yarn around the loom one and a half times; cut the yarn.

2. Using a yarn needle, thread the working yarn through each loop on the loom. Start with the loop to the left of the holding peg and work in a clockwise direction all the way around the loom, **Photo 8**.

Photo 8

3. Thread the working yarn through the loop to the left of the holding peg a second time.

4. Remove the loops from the loom and gently tug on the yarn tail until the piece gathers tightly together, **Photo 9**. Using the needle, secure the working yarn on the inside of the piece.

Photo 9

5. Turn the piece inside out and weave in the ends.

Flat Piece Method

1. Work piece until desired length as directed in pattern, ending with your working yarn at the right next to the holding peg. Cut the working yarn leaving a 3-inch tail.

2. Starting at the side of the piece with your working yarn, take the last loop from its peg and place it on the knitting tool or crochet hook.

3. Take the working yarn and wrap it once around the knitting tool or crochet hook in a clockwise direction. Pull this loop through the loop already on the crochet hook.

4. Remove the loop from the next peg to the right and place it on the hook, **Photo 10**.

Photo 10

5. Pull the second loop through the first and slide the first loop off the hook.

6. Repeat from step 3 and continue until all loops are removed from the loom.

7. After removing the last loop from the loom, use your hook to pull the tail of working yarn through it. Weave in ends with yarn needle.

Tube Method

1. Work piece until desired length as directed in pattern. Cut your working yarn leaving a 3-inch tail.

2. Start at the peg just to the right of the holding peg. Remove the loop from its peg and place it on the knitting tool or crochet hook.

3. Remove the loop from the next peg to the right and place it on the hook.

4. Pull the second loop through the first and slide the first loop off the hook.

5. Remove the next loop to the right and repeat.

6. Continue in this manner until all loops are removed from the loom.

7. After removing the last loop from the loom, use your hook to pull the tail of working yarn through it. Weave in ends with yarn needle.

Note: *You can make the tube looser if you use a crochet hook and make one chain stitch between each loomed stitch as in the Flat Piece Method.*

Flat Closed Method

1. Work piece until desired length as directed in pattern. Cut yarn leaving a 3-inch tail.

2. Thread a yarn needle with a piece of yarn in the main color (MC) around 1–2 yards in length.

3. Starting at the peg indicated in the pattern, thread the yarn up through that loop, **Photo 11**, and remove it from its peg.

Note: *A contrasting yarn color was used in Photo 11 for illustration purposes only.*

4. Move to the peg just to the left of the first loop removed. Thread the yarn through this loop as well and remove from the loom.

5. Next move to the peg just to the right of the first loop removed. Thread the yarn through this loop and remove it.

Photo 11

6. Continue to alternate left to right across the loom threading the yarn through the next peg and removing it from the loom until all the loops are removed from the loom.

7. Once all the loops are removed, gently pull the yarn through the loops being sure not to gather the piece.

8. Thread the end of the yarn through the corner and inside the pieces. Turn the piece inside out and secure the end. Weave in ends with yarn needle.

Making a Brim or Cuff

1. Knit in the round as many rows as directed by your pattern.

2. Reach inside and pull up the first row of cast-on stitches. These will tend to be looser than the other stitches.

3. Starting with the first peg, place the loops from the cast-on edge on each peg of the loom, **Photo 12**.

Photo 12

Make sure that each peg has two loops.

4. Knit off pegs by pulling the bottom loop up and over the one you just placed on the peg.

5. Wrap and continue to knit as directed in the pattern.

Note: *The first row after bringing the brim up will be very tight.*

Changing Colors

1. Cut yarn of first color leaving a 3-inch tail.

2. Form a slip knot leaving a 3-inch tail on the end of the new color yarn.

3. Place the slip knot over the holding peg or on the empty peg available on the loom.

4. Wrap and knit with the new color of yarn as directed in the pattern.

5. Remove the slip knot from its peg once three to four rows have been knit.

Shaping Pieces

Sometimes a pattern calls for increasing stitches and decreasing stitches to shape a piece. This is very easy to do.

Increasing One Stitch per Row

1. Take the loop on the end of the row you want to increase and lift it off its peg, placing it on the next peg away from the main part of the row. This will leave an empty peg between your main row and the peg with the loop you just moved, **Photo 13**.

Photo 13

2. Wrap all pegs including the empty peg and knit off all pegs with two loops. On the next row, that peg will have two loops and will be knit off with the rest of the row.

Increasing More Than One Stitch per Row

1. Wrap the number of pegs called for on the next empty pegs at the end of your row.

2. Knit off the loops on the main row then turn and wrap all the pegs including the extra pegs and knit off.

Decreasing One Stitch per Row

1. Take the loop on second peg in from the end of the row you wish to decrease. Place it on the third peg in from the end of the row, **Photo 14**.

Photo 14

2. Move the loop on the last peg in the row to the peg that was left empty by the one that was removed.

3. Wrap all the pegs that have loops on them; the decrease peg will have three loops on it.

4. Knit off all pegs. When knitting off the decrease peg, take the two bottom loops and pull them up and over the top loop and over and off the peg.

Decreasing More Than One Stitch per Row

1. Take the last loop on the end you wish to decrease off its peg and place it on the next one in.

2. Pull the bottom loop up and through the upper loop as if purling, removing the upper loop from the peg, **Photo 15**.

Photo 15

3. Repeat steps 1 and 2 until desired number of stitches are bound off, placing the last loop on the next peg in.

4. Wrap all pegs with loops remaining on them. The last peg will have three loops.

5. Knit off all pegs. Knit off the last peg by lifting the bottom two loops up and over the top loop.

I-Cords

I-cords make great handles for bags and can be used as edges for throws or blankets as well. They are very easy to do on a knitting loom.

1. Cast on and wrap number of pegs as indicated in your pattern.

2. Turn and wrap them as for knitting a flat piece and knit off.

3. Take the end of the working yarn behind the pegs from the peg on the right and over to the last peg on the left, **Photo 16**.

Photo 16

4. Wrap the pegs from left to right and knit off starting with the last loop wrapped. Pull down on your work to set the stitches, **Photo 17**.

Photo 17

5. Continue in this manner until the I-cord is the desired length. Bind off following the Flat Piece Method (see page 7).

EASY

Size

Woman's small (medium, large). Instructions are given for smallest size, with larger sizes in parentheses. When only 1 number is given, it applies to all sizes.

Finished Measurement

Chest: 36 (40, 44) inches

Materials

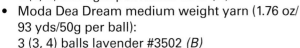

- Red Heart Super Saver medium weight yarn (7 oz/364 yds/198g per ball):
  1 (1, 2) ball light periwinkle #347 *(A)*
- Moda Dea Dream medium weight yarn (1.76 oz/ 93 yds/50g per ball):
  3 (3, 4) balls lavender #3502 *(B)*
- Yellow Knifty Knitter circle loom with 41 pegs
- Knitting tool or crochet hook
- Tapestry needle
- Safety pins

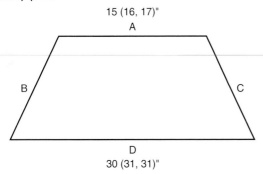

15 (16, 17)"
A
B   C
D
30 (31, 31)"

Fig. 1

Gauge

10 stitches and 8 rows = 4 inches in Stockinette stitch
Be sure to check gauge.

Stitches Used

Stockinette Stitch: Knit every round.
Chain Stitch: Yarn over knitting tool or crochet hook, draw loop through loop on hook.

Instructions

Front/Back

Make 2.

1. Starting on the first peg to the left of the holding peg and with 1 strand of A and B held together, cast on 3 stitches. Knit 2 rows in **Stockinette stitch** *(see Stitches Used)*.

2. Wrap pegs 4–6 as for a flat piece and wrap pegs 6–1 and knit off.

3. *Knit 1 row. Wrap 3 more pegs and turn as for a flat piece. Wrap all pegs and knit off. Repeat from * until there are 39 pegs in use.

4. Mark the stitch on peg 39 with a piece of waste yarn or safety pin. Knit even until the piece measures 15 (16, 17) inches from the marked stitch. End on the peg just to the left of the holding peg.

5. Wrap and knit 36 stitches. Turn and wrap the same stitches and knit off.

6. Continue in this manner reducing the number of stitches by 3 every other row until only 3 stitches are wrapped. Knit those 3 stitches off ending at peg 1. Cut yarn.

Finishing

7. Using knitting tool or crochet hook, remove the piece from the loom by binding off following the Flat Piece Method (see page 7), making 1 **Chain stitch** *(see Stitches Used)* between each loom stitch for a looser edge.

8. To seam, place the 2 pieces right sides together with edge B of 1 piece and edge C of the other together. Using 1 strand of A and yarn needle, work your way back and forth up the edges of the 2 pieces, catching a bump on the edge of each piece, alternating sides. This makes a smooth invisible seam. Repeat for the other side.

9. Weave in all ends.

At-Home-Comfort Socks

INTERMEDIATE

Sizes

Woman's shoe size 5/6 (7/8, 9/10). Instructions are given for smallest size, with larger sizes in parentheses. When only 1 number is given it applies to all sizes.

Materials

- Wool-Ease Chunky bulky weight yarn (5 oz/153 yds/140g per ball): 2 (2, 2) balls bluebell #107 *(A)* 1 (1, 1) ball deep rose #140 *(B)*
- Blue Knifty Knitter circle loom with 24 pegs
- Knitting tool or crochet hook
- Tapestry needle

Gauge

12 stitches and 15 rows = 4 inches in Stockinette stitch Be sure to check gauge.

Stitches Used

Ribbing Pattern: Knit 1 stitch, purl 1 stitch on all rows.
Stockinette Stitch: Knit every round.

Instructions

Cuff

With A, cast on all 24 pegs.

Work **Ribbing Pattern** *(see Stitches Used)* for 33 rows.

Cut A. Join B.

Turning the Heel

Row 1: Wrap and knit pegs 1–12 in Ribbing Pattern.

Row 2: Turn as for a flat piece, wrap and knit the same stitches.

Row 3: Wrap pegs 2–11 and knit off.

Row 4: Turn as for flat piece, wrap and knit the same stitches.

Row 5: Wrap and knit pegs 3–10.

Row 6: Turn as for a flat piece, wrap and knit the same stitches.

Row 7: Wrap and knit pegs 4–9.

Row 8: Turn as for a flat piece, wrap and knit the same stitches.

From the inside of the sock, lift a stitch from the 2nd row below peg 3 and place it on peg 4 (see photo). Lift a stitch from below peg 10 and place it on peg 9.

Row 9: Wrap pegs 4–9 and knit off, being sure to lift the 2 bottom loops over from the pegs that have 3 loops.

Row 10: Turn as for a flat piece, wrap and knit the same stitches.

From the inside of the sock, lift a stitch from the 2nd row below peg 2 and place it on peg 3. Lift a stitch from below peg 11 and place it on peg 10.

Row 11: Wrap pegs 3–10 and knit off, being sure to lift the 2 bottom loops over from the pegs that have 3 loops.

From the inside of the sock lift a stitch from the 2nd row below peg 1 and place it on peg 2. Lift a stitch from below peg 12 and place it on peg 11.

Row 12: Wrap pegs 2–11 and knit off, being sure to lift the 2 bottom loops over from the pegs that have 3 loops.

Row 13: Turn as for a flat piece, wrap and knit the same stitches.

From the inside of the sock, lift a stitch from the 2nd row below peg 24 and place it on peg 1. Lift a stitch from below peg 13 and place it on peg 12.

Row 14: Wrap pegs 1–12 and knit off, being sure to lift the 2 bottom loops over from the pegs that have 3 loops.

Row 15: Turn as for a flat piece, wrap and knit the same stitches.

Cut B, leaving a 3-inch tail. Join A.

Foot

Wrap and knit pegs 1–12.

Wrap and knit pegs 13–24 in Ribbing Pattern.

Knit 14 (17, 20) rows.

Cut A, leaving a 3-inch tail. Join B.

Toe Bottom

Row 1: Wrap and knit pegs 1–12.

Row 2: Turn as for a flat piece, wrap and knit the same stitches.

Row 3: Wrap and knit pegs 2–11.

Row 4: Turn as for a flat piece, wrap and knit the same stitches.

Row 5: Wrap and knit pegs 3–10.

Row 6: Turn as for a flat piece, wrap and knit the same stitches.

Row 7: Wrap and knit pegs 4–9.

Row 8: Turn as for a flat piece, wrap and knit the same stitches.

Cut B, leaving a 3-inch tail.

Toe Top

Row 1: Rejoin B; wrap and knit pegs 13–24.

Row 2: Turn as for a flat piece, wrap and knit the same stitches.

Row 3: Wrap and knit pegs 14–23.

Row 4: Turn as for a flat piece, wrap and knit the same stitches.

Row 5: Wrap and knit pegs 15–22.

Row 6: Turn as for a flat piece, wrap and knit the same stitches.

Row 7: Wrap and knit pegs 16–21.

Row 8: Turn as for a flat piece, wrap and knit the same stitches.

Cut B, leaving a 36-inch tail.

Finishing

To seam the toe, follow the Flat Closed Method on page 8.

Weave in all ends.

Mom & Daughter Bangle Bags

BEGINNER

Size

Small (large). Instructions are given for small (daughter) size, with large (mom) size in parentheses. When only 1 number is given it applies to both sizes.

Finished Measurement

4 x 5 inches (7 x 8 inches)

Materials

- Lion Brand Jiffy bulky weight yarn (3 oz/135 yds/85g per ball): 1 ball denim #107 *(A)*
- Lion Brand Fun Fur bulky weight yarn (1½ oz/ 57 yds/40g per ball): 1 ball citrus #207 *(B)*
- Blue Knifty Knitter circle loom 24 pegs (or Green Knifty Knitter circle loom 36 pegs)
- Knitting tool or crochet hook
- Tapestry needle
- 1 pair 3-inch bangle bracelets (or 1 pair purse handles of your choice, maximum 6 inches in round)

5 BULKY

Gauge

13 stitches and 12 rows (12 stitches and 14 rows) = 4 inches in Stockinette stitch.
Be sure to check gauge.

Stitch Used

Stockinette Stitch: Knit every round.

Instructions

1. With A, cast on pegs 1–12 (1–18) and knit as a flat piece.

2. Knit 6 (10) rows. Cut A, leaving a 3-inch tail.

3. With A, cast on pegs 13–24 (19–36) and knit as a flat piece.

4. Knit 6 (10) rows. Cut A leaving a 3-inch tail.

5. On next row, wrap all pegs with A and knit off.

Adding Handles

6. Working with the half-knit stitches on pegs 1–12 (1–18), place the handles on the inside of the loom. Bring the cast-on row up through the inside of the handle as for a hat brim and place the loops on the corresponding pegs. Knit off.

7. Repeat step 5 on pegs 13–24 (19–36).

8. Join B and start knitting in the round.

9. Knit until the piece measures 4 (7) inches long. Cut B, leaving a 3-inch tail.

10. Cut A, leaving a 3-yard tail.

11. Bind off following the Flat Closed Method (see page 8) and using A to close the bottom.

12. Turn piece inside out. This is the right side. Fluff up B.

13. Weave in all ends.

Make-It-Soft Scarf

EASY

Size
One size

Finished Measurement
8 x 54 inches

Materials
- Lion Brand Suede bulky weight yarn
  (3 oz/122 yds/85g per ball):
  2 balls olive #210
- Yellow Knifty Knitter circle loom with 41 pegs
- Knitting tool or crochet hook
- Yarn needle

5 BULKY

Gauge
12 stitches and 15 rows = 4 inches in Garter stitch
Be sure to check gauge.

Stitches Used
Garter Stitch: Purl 1 row, knit 1 row.
Border Edge Pattern:
Row 1: Purl 3 stitches, knit 18 stitches, purl 3 stitches.
Row 2: Knit all stitches.
Chain Stitch: Yarn over knitting tool or crochet hook,
  draw loop through loop on hook.

Instructions

1. Cast on 24 pegs. Turn as for flat piece and purl the first row.

2. Continue in **Garter stitch** *(see Stitches Used)* for 10 rows, ending on a knit row.

3. Begin **Border Edge Pattern** *(see Stitches Used)*.

4. Continue in Border Edge Pattern until the scarf reaches 52 inches or desired length, ending on row 2.

5. Work Garter stitch for 10 rows.

6. Using knitting tool or crochet hook, bind off following the Flat Piece Method (see page 7), making 1 **Chain stitch** *(see Stitches Used)* between each loom stitch.

7. Weave in ends.

Make-It-Soft Hat

INTERMEDIATE

Size
Adult

Finished Measurement
8 x 22 inches

Materials
- Lion Brand Suede bulky weight yarn (3 oz/122 yds/85g per skein): 1 skein olive #210
- Yellow Knifty Knitter circle loom with 41 pegs
- Knitting tool or crochet hook
- Yarn needle

5 BULKY

Gauge
8 stitches and 14 rows = 4 inches in Stockinette stitch
Be sure to check gauge.

Stitches Used
Garter Stitch: Purl 1 row, knit 1 row.
Stockinette Stitch: Knit every round.

Instructions

Brim
1. Cast on using all pegs.

2. Work **Garter stitch** *(see Stitches Used)* for 12 rows, ending on a knit row.

3. Knit 11 rows.

Crown
1. The loops on the loom will be divided into 4 groups of 10. Take the loop from the peg just to the right of the starting peg and place it on next peg to the right. Knit off.

Row 1: Wrap pegs 40–31 and knit off.

Row 2: Turn and wrap the same pegs and knit off.

* Using pegs 40–31, number them from 1–10, left to right and continue.

Row 3: Take the loop from peg 1 and move it to peg 2. Take the loop from peg 10 and move it to peg 9. Wrap all pegs and knit off. Be sure to lift off the 2 bottom loops on the pegs that have 3 loops. There will be 8 stitches left.

Row 4: Turn and wrap the same pegs and knit off.

Row 5: Take the loop from peg 2 and move it to peg 3. Take the loop from peg 9 and move it to peg 8. Knit off. Be sure to lift off the 2 bottom loops on the pegs that have 3 loops. Wrap all pegs and knit off. There will be 6 stitches left.

Row 6: Turn as for a flat piece, wrap and knit the same stitches.

Row 7: Take the loop from peg 3 and move it to peg 4. Take the loop from peg 8 and move it to peg 7. Knit off. Be sure to lift off the 2 bottom loops on the pegs that have 3 loops. Wrap all pegs and knit off. There will be 4 stitches left.

Row 8: Turn as for a flat piece, wrap and knit the same stitches.

Row 9: Take the loop from peg 4 and move it to peg 5. Take the loop from peg 7 and move it to peg 6. Knit off. Be sure to lift off the 2 bottom loops on the pegs that have 3 loops. Wrap all pegs and knit off. There will be 2 stitches left.

Row 10: Turn as for a flat piece, wrap and knit the same stitches.

Row 11: Take the loop from peg 5 and place it on peg 6. Cut yarn, leaving a 3-inch tail. Pull the tail through the loop on peg 6 and remove the loop from the peg.

2. Move on to pegs 30–21. Place your working yarn on peg 30 and wrap pegs 30–21. Turn as for a flat piece and knit off. Beginning at *, repeat crown shaping pattern.

3. Move on to pegs 20–11 and place your working yarn on peg 20 and wrap pegs 20–11. Turn as for a flat piece and knit off. Beginning at *, repeat crown shaping pattern.

4. Move on to pegs 10–1 and place your working yarn on peg 10 and wrap pegs 10–1. Turn as for a flat piece and knit off. Beginning at *, repeat crown shaping pattern.

Finishing
5. Turn the hat inside out. Line up the edges of the crown and join with mattress stitch (see page 30).

6. Weave in all ends.

Striped Squares Baby Blanket

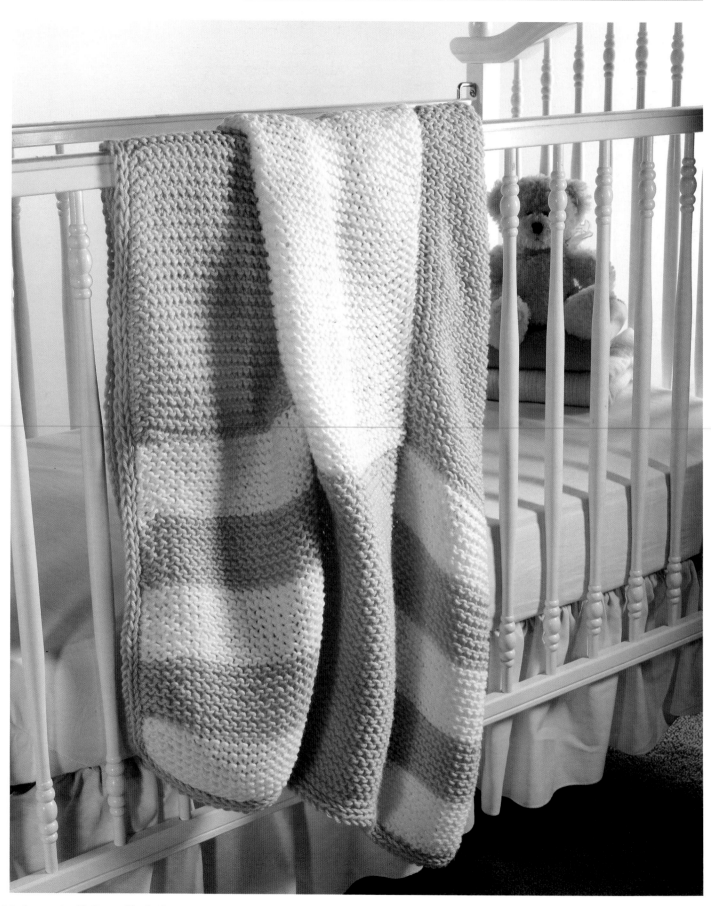

EASY

Size

One size

Finished Measurement

34 x 44 inches

Materials

- Lion Brand Jaime Classic medium weight yarn (2½ oz/116yds/78g per ball):
  3 balls snow #100 (B)
  6 balls candy blue #106 (A)
- Yellow Knifty Knitter circle loom with 41 pegs
- Knitting tool or crochet hook
- Yarn needle

Gauge

19 stitches and 22 rows = 4 inches in Garter stitch. Be sure to check gauge.

Stitches Used

Garter Stitch: Purl 1 row, knit 1 row.
Chain Stitch: Yarn over knitting tool or crochet hook, draw loop through loop on hook.

Instructions

Strip 1

Make 2.

Section 1

1. With B, cast on 27 pegs.

2. Work in **Garter stitch** (see Stitches Used).

3. Knit 15 rows.

4. Cut B, leaving a 3-inch tail.

5. Join A. Knit 14 rows.

6. Cut A, leaving a 3-inch tail.

7. Join B. Knit 16 rows.

8. Cut B, leaving a 3-inch tail.

9. Join A. Knit 14 rows.

10. Cut A, leaving a 3-inch tail.

11. Join B. Knit 15 rows.

12. Cut B, leaving a 3-inch tail.

Section 2

13. Join A. Knit 75 rows.

14. Cut A, leaving a 3-inch tail.

15. Repeat Section 1.

16. Using knitting tool or crochet hook, bind off following the Flat Piece Method (see page 7), making 1 **Chain stitch** (see Stitches Used) between each loom stitch.

17. Weave in ends.

Strip 2

Make 1.

18. With A, cast on 27 pegs.

19. Work in Garter stitch.

20. Knit 74 rows.

21. Cut A, leaving a 3-inch tail.

22. Join B. Knit 75 rows.

23. Cut B, leaving a 3-inch tail.

24. Join A. Knit 75 rows.

25. Bind off in same manner as Strip 1.

26. Weave in ends.

I-Cord Edging

27. Make a 4-stitch I-cord (see page 10) 160 inches long.

28. Join the I-cord edging around the edge with mattress stitch (see page 30). Take care not to twist the cording as you join it.

29. Weave in ends.

Finishing

30. Referring to diagram for placement, arrange the strips. Join together using mattress stitch (see page 30).

31. Join the I-cord edging around the edge with mattress stitch. Take care not to twist the cording as you join.

31. Weave in ends.

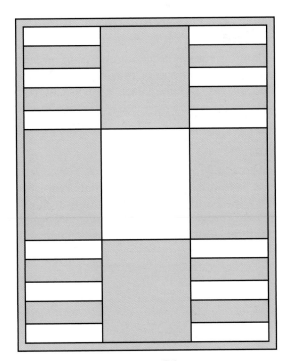

Placement Diagram

Keep-Warm Tubular Scarf

BEGINNER

Size

One size

Finished Measurement

4 x 53 inches without fringe

Materials

- Caron Jewel Box medium weight yarn (2½oz/90 yds/70.9g per ball): 2 balls rubellite #0028
- Blue Knifty Knitter circle loom with 24 pegs
- Knitting tool
- Crochet hook
- Yarn needle

Gauge

12 stitches and 16 rows = 4 inches in Stockinette stitch
Be sure to check gauge.

Stitches Used

Stockinette Stitch: Knit every row.
Chain Stitch: Yarn over knitting tool or crochet hook, draw loop through loop on hook.

Instructions

1. Cast on all pegs.

2. Knit in the round in **Stockinette stitch** (see Stitches Used) until piece reaches the desired length.

3. Using knitting tool or crochet hook, bind off following the Tube Method (see page 7), making 1 **Chain stitch** (see Stitches Used) between each loom knit stitch.

4. Weave in ends.

Finishing

5. For fringe, cut 6-inch lengths of yarn. For each knot of fringe, use 3 strands. Fold strands in half. With crochet hook, pull folded end from back to front through first stitch on 1 short end of scarf. Draw ends through folded end and tighten knot. Repeat in each stitch across each short end. Trim ends.

Keep-Warm Hat

BEGINNER

Size

Youth (adult)
Instructions are given for smallest size, with larger size in parentheses. When only 1 number is given, it applies to all sizes.

Finished Measurements

9 x 21 (9 x 22) inches

Materials

- Caron Jewel Box medium weight yarn (2½ oz/100 yds/71g per skein): 3 skeins rubellite #0028
- Green Knifty Knitter circle loom with 36 pegs (or Yellow Knifty Knitter circle loom with 41 pegs)
- Knitting tool or crochet hook
- Yarn needle

Gauge

10 stitches and 15 rows = 4 inches in Stockinette stitch
Be sure to check gauge.

Stitch Used

Stockinette Stitch: Knit every row.

Instructions

1. With 2 strands of yarn held together, cast on using all pegs.

2. Knit in the round in **Stockinette stitch** *(see Stitch Used)* until the piece measures 4 inches long.

3. Pull up from the center of the loom the stitches from the cast-on edge. Place on pegs. There should be 2 loops on each peg. Knit off all pegs.

Note: *Following row will be tight.*

4. Wrap all pegs with your working yarn and knit off.

5. Continue knitting in the round until the piece measures 9 inches long.

6. Cut yarn, leaving a 36-inch tail.

7. Bind off following the Gather Method (see page 6).

8. Weave in ends.

Relaxing Afghan

EASY

Size

48 x 54 inches

Materials

- Red Heart Super Saver medium weight yarn (7 oz/364 yds/198g per skein): 5 skeins each dark sage #633 *(A)* and medium sage #632 *(B)* 4 skeins aran #313 *(C)*
- Yellow Knifty Knitter circle loom with 41 pegs
- Knitting tool
- Crochet hook
- Yarn needle

Gauge

10 stitches and 13 rows = 4 inches in Stockinette stitch
Be sure to check gauge.

Stitches Used

Stockinette Stitch: Knit every row.
Chain Stitch: Yarn over knitting tool or crochet hook, draw loop through loop on hook.

Instructions

Note: Use 2 strands of yarn held together throughout.

Strip 1

Make 2.

1. With A, cast on 23 pegs. Knit 39 rows.
2. Cut A, leaving a 3-inch tail.
3. Join B. Knit 39 rows.
4. Cut B, leaving a 3-inch tail.
5. Join C. Knit 39 rows.
6. Cut C, leaving a 3-inch tail.
7. Join B. Knit 39 rows.
8. Cut B, leaving a 3-inch tail.
9. Join A. Knit 39 rows.

10. Using knitting tool or crochet hook, bind off following the Flat Piece Method (see page 7), making 1 **Chain stitch** *(see Stitches Used)* between each loomed stitch.
11. Cut A, leaving a 3-inch tail.
12. Weave in ends.

Strip 2

Make 2.

13. Using B, cast on. Knit 39 rows.
14. Cut B, leaving a 3-inch tail.
15. Join C. Knit 39 rows.
16. Cut C, leaving a 3-inch tail.
17. Join A. Knit 39 rows.
18. Cut A, leaving a 3-inch tail.
19. Join C. Knit 39 rows.
20. Cut C, leaving a 3-inch tail.
21. Join B. Knit 39 rows.
22. Bind off in same manner as Strip 1.
23. Cut B, leaving a 3-inch tail.
24. Weave in ends.

Strip 3

Make 1.

25. With C, cast on 23 pegs. Knit 39 rows.
26. Cut C, leaving a 3-inch tail.
27. Join A. Knit 39 rows.
28. Cut A, leaving a 3-inch tail.
29. Join B. Knit 39 rows.
30. Cut B, leaving a 3-inch tail.
31. Join A. Knit 39 rows.
32. Cut A, leaving a 3-inch tail.
33. Join C. Knit 39 rows.
34. Bind off in same manner as Strip 1.
35. Cut C, leaving a 3-inch tail.
36. Weave in ends.

Finishing

37. Referring to diagram for placement, arrange Strips. Join together using mattress stitch (Fig. 1).

Fringe

38. For fringe, cut 8-inch lengths of A, B and C. For each knot of fringe, use 1 strand of each color. Fold strands in half. With crochet hook, draw folded end from back to front through first stitch on 1 short end of afghan. Draw ends through folded end and tighten knot. Tie knots in every other stitch across each short end of afghan. Trim ends.

Fig. 1, Mattress Stitch

Placement Diagram

Skill Levels

Metric Chart

INCHES INTO MILLIMETERS & CENTIMETERS (Rounded off slightly)

inches	mm	cm	inches	cm	inches	cm	inches	cm
1/8	3	0.3	5	12.5	21	53.5	38	96.5
1/4	6	0.6	5 1/2	14	22	56	39	99
3/8	10	1	6	15	23	58.5	40	101.5
1/2	13	1.3	7	18	24	61	41	104
5/8	15	1.5	8	20.5	25	63.5	42	106.5
3/4	20	2	9	23	26	66	43	109
7/8	22	2.2	10	25.5	27	68.5	44	112
1	25	2.5	11	28	28	71	45	114.5
1 1/4	32	3.2	12	30.5	29	73.5	46	117
1 1/2	38	3.8	13	33	30	76	47	119.5
1 3/4	45	4.5	14	35.5	31	79	48	122
2	50	5	15	38	32	81.5	49	124.5
2 1/2	65	6.5	16	40.5	33	84	50	127
3	75	7.5	17	43	34	86.5		
3 1/2	90	9	18	46	35	89		
4	100	10	19	48.5	36	91.5		
4 1/2	115	11.5	20	51	37	94		

Standard Yarn Weight System

Yarn Weight Symbol & Category Names	1 SUPER FINE	2 FINE	3 LIGHT	4 MEDIUM	5 BULKY	6 SUPER BULKY
Type of Yarns in Category	Sock, Fingering, Baby	Sport, Baby	DK, Light Worsted	Worsted, Afghan, Aran	Chunky, Craft, Rug	Bulky, Roving
Knit Gauge Range* in Stockinette Stitch to 4 inches	27–32 sts	23–26 sts	21–24 sts	16–20 sts	12–15 sts	6–11 sts

* GUIDELINES ONLY: The above reflect the most commonly used gauges for specific yarn categories.

We wish to thank the following companies for supplying products for the projects:
Kniffy Knitter Looms: Provo Craft
Yarns: Caron, Coats & Clark and Lion Brand Yarns

Annie's ™ *Learn to Knit on Circle Looms* is published by Annie's, 306 East Parr Road, Berne, IN 46711. Printed in USA. Copyright © 2006, 2013 Annie's. All rights reserved. This publication may not be reproduced in part or in whole without written permission from the publisher.

RETAIL STORES: If you would like to carry this pattern book or any other Annie's publication, visit AnniesWSL.com.

Every effort has been made to ensure that the instructions in this pattern book are complete and accurate. We cannot, however, take responsibility for human error, typographical mistakes or variations in individual work. Please visit AnniesCustomerCare.com to check for pattern updates.

ISBN: 978-1-59012-158-0
24 25 26 27 28 29 30